FONDUE COOKBOOK FOR BEGINNERS

Step-by-Step Cheese and Chocolate Recipes You'll Love

GRAPEVINE BOOKS

Published by

GRAPEVINE BOOKS

www.grapevinebooks.com

email: contact@grapevinebooks.com

Ordering Information:

Quantity sales: Special discounts are available on quantity purchases by corporations, associations, and others.

For details, reach out to the publisher.

First published by Grapevine Books, 2025

Contents

Get Your Free E-book

Get Your Free E-book
Scan the QR code below to instantly access the e-book
'The Fondue Host's Cheat Sheet', absolutely free

SCAN ME

https://bonus.grapevinebooks.com/fonduecheatsheet

Introduction

The Warm, Shared Magic of Fondue

Fondue isn't just a dish. It's an experience. A pot at the center of the table, warm and bubbling, invites everyone to gather close, take a skewer, and dip into something delicious. Whether it's cheese, chocolate, oil, or broth, fondue transforms ordinary meals into memorable moments. It's food meant for sharing, laughter, and lingering. But where did it come from, and why has it remained a favorite for centuries?

The word "fondue" comes from the French word *fondre*, meaning "to melt," and at its core, that's what fondue is all about—melting food into something creamy, smooth, and perfect for dipping. Although most people think of fondue as a Swiss invention, its story winds through the Alps, French kitchens, and even postwar America. Like the best dishes, it evolved from simple, practical roots into a beloved culinary tradition.

A Brief History of Fondue

Fondue's origin story begins in the rugged alpine regions of Switzerland. In the 18th century, rural Swiss families faced long winters with limited fresh food. What they did have, though, was cheese—often aged and hardened. Melting it with a bit of wine over the fire created a warm, hearty meal that could be shared by the entire family. Stale bread, too hard to eat alone, became the perfect tool for dipping. This resourceful meal eventually became a staple of mountain life and, later, a symbol of Swiss national pride.

As fondue became popular across Switzerland, local variations emerged. The French-speaking regions preferred Gruyère cheese, while others blended Emmental or added wine, garlic, or kirsch (a cherry brandy). By the early 20th century, fondue had taken on a national identity. In fact, during World War II, the Swiss Cheese Union launched a campaign promoting cheese fondue as a patriotic dish to unite the country—and sell more cheese.

Fondue's rise to international fame, however, came in the 1950s and 60s. At the 1964 New York World's Fair, the Swiss Pavilion featured a fondue demonstration that captivated American audiences. In the decades that followed, fondue sets became a popular wedding gift, and fondue parties—a mix of food and social fun—swept through homes in the U.S. and beyond. What was once a humble alpine meal became a global phenomenon.

The Four Main Types of Fondue

Today, fondue comes in many forms, and each type brings its own flair and flavor. Here are the four main categories you'll encounter in this book:

1. Cheese Fondue

This is the original classic. Rich, creamy, and deeply satisfying, cheese fondue combines melted cheese with wine, garlic, and other flavorings. Traditional Swiss versions like *moitié-moitié* (half Gruyère, half Vacherin) are joined by creative takes using cheddar, brie, blue cheese, or even spicy pepper jack. Bread cubes are the classic dipper, but apples, broccoli, roasted potatoes, and sausage also pair beautifully.

2. Chocolate Fondue

Introduced later but no less beloved, chocolate fondue brings a dessert twist to the tradition. Melted milk, dark, or white chocolate—sometimes infused with cream, liqueur, or fruit zest—forms the base. Marshmallows, strawberries, bananas, pretzels, and cookies all find their way into the pot. It's romantic, playful, and perfect for date nights or celebrations.

3. Broth Fondue (Fondue Chinoise)

Instead of cheese or chocolate, this version uses a hot, seasoned broth. Thin slices of meat, vegetables, or tofu are cooked directly in the simmering liquid. Once cooked, the pieces are dipped in flavorful sauces. Broth fondues are lighter and great for those seeking a healthier or more interactive dinner experience.

4. Oil Fondue (Fondue Bourguignonne)

Popularized in France, this version uses hot oil to cook bite-sized pieces of meat, poultry, or seafood. Once golden and crisp, they're dipped into sauces like aioli, mustard, or horseradish cream. This fondue is festive, hearty, and ideal for dinner parties, though it does require careful attention for safety.

Why Fondue Still Matters

In an age of fast meals and solo dining, fondue reminds us to slow down, gather, and enjoy food together. It encourages conversation, playfulness, and creativity. The ingredients are simple, but the results are rich with connection.

This book will guide you through 60 delicious fondue recipes—from classic Swiss cheese to decadent chocolate desserts, from savory broths to sizzling oil dips. You'll learn step-by-step how to set up, cook, serve, and enjoy each one, no matter your experience level.

So light the burner, grab your skewers, and get ready to dip into something special. Fondue is waiting—and everyone's invited.

Basic Ingredients & Sourcing Them

When it comes to fondue, the ingredients may be simple, but quality matters. Since fondue focuses on just a few main elements, using fresh, flavorful ingredients makes a huge difference. Let's break down the key components you'll need for cheese, chocolate, broth, and oil fondues—and how to source them confidently.

Cheese Fondue Ingredients

The star of cheese fondue is, of course, the cheese. Traditional Swiss blends typically use:

- **Gruyère** – Smooth, nutty, and slightly salty
- **Emmental** – Mild with a hint of sweetness
- **Appenzeller** – Stronger and more aromatic

These are available at well-stocked supermarkets, especially in the cheese or deli section. If unavailable, try specialty cheese shops or online retailers. For easier versions, cheddar, gouda, fontina, and havarti are great alternatives.

Other essentials include:

- **Dry white wine** – For flavor and to help the cheese melt smoothly (Pinot Grigio or Sauvignon Blanc work well)

- **Garlic** – Rubbed into the pot or minced for deeper flavor
- **Cornstarch** – Helps thicken and stabilize the cheese mixture
- **Lemon juice** – A splash aids in melting and brightens the flavor
- **Kirsch (cherry brandy)** – Optional, adds a hint of fruitiness

Chocolate Fondue Ingredients

Chocolate fondue is all about indulgence. You'll need:

- **Chocolate** – Use high-quality bars or chips. Dark, milk, or white—choose what you love.
- **Heavy cream** – For smooth richness
- **Butter** – Optional, adds a silkier texture
- **Vanilla extract** – Enhances flavor
- **Salt** – Just a pinch to balance sweetness
- **Flavor add-ins** – Liqueurs (like Grand Marnier, Baileys), espresso powder, citrus zest, or spices like cinnamon can elevate your fondue

Most of these can be found in the baking aisle. When selecting chocolate, skip the candy bars and go for baking chocolate or couverture (sold in chunks or discs).

Broth & Oil Fondue Ingredients

These fondues are great for cooking meat, seafood, and vegetables.

For **broth fondue**, you'll need:

- **Broth base** – Chicken, beef, vegetable, or seafood broth (homemade or boxed)
- **Aromatics** – Garlic, onion, ginger, herbs like thyme or parsley
- **Acid or wine** – A splash of soy sauce, vinegar, or wine deepens flavor

For **oil fondue**, choose:

- **Neutral oils** – Canola, peanut, or sunflower oil with high smoke points
- **Fresh herbs or spices** – Optional, for flavor infusion

Make sure to buy lean, thin-sliced meats (like beef tenderloin or chicken breast), deveined shrimp, and firm vegetables. Pre-sliced stir-fry meat packs from grocery stores are often ideal for fondue.

Dippers and Sides

Each fondue type benefits from a spread of "dippers":

- **Bread** – Cubed baguette, sourdough, or rye
- **Fruit** – Apples, pears, strawberries, bananas, grapes
- **Veggies** – Blanched broccoli, baby carrots, cherry tomatoes, mushrooms
- **Sweets** – Marshmallows, cookies, pound cake, pretzels

When sourcing dippers, freshness is key. Use local produce, or visit farmer's markets for seasonal variety.

Where to Shop

- **Local supermarkets** – Most carry the basics (cheddar, chocolate, cream, broth, wine, bread)
- **Cheese shops** – Great for Swiss cheeses or specialty items
- **International markets** – For harder-to-find items like kirsch or unique oils
- **Online retailers** – Ideal for specialty chocolates, fondue-specific tools, or bulk items

Buy only what you need for one fondue night to keep things fresh. If you're planning a party, prep ingredients a day ahead, store them in airtight containers, and arrange your dipping station before guests arrive.

Fondue Equipment & Safety

Fondue is as much about the tools as the food. Having the right equipment ensures smooth melting, easy dipping, and a safe, enjoyable experience.

Essential Equipment

1. **Fondue Pot (Caquelon)**

2. The centerpiece of the fondue experience. Choose one based on the type of fondue:

- **Ceramic or earthenware** – Best for cheese and chocolate. Retains gentle, even heat.
- **Stainless steel or metal** – Ideal for broth or oil fondues that need higher temperatures.
- **Electric fondue pots** – Offer precise temperature control for all fondue types.
- **Tea light sets** – Good for keeping cheese or chocolate warm after melting on the stove.

2. **Fuel Source**

- **Tea lights** – Safe for keeping warm fondue going at the table.
- **Sterno burners or gel fuel** – Used for oil or broth, but require caution.
- **Electric base** – Easiest for beginners and safer than open flames.

3. Fondue Forks or Skewers

Use color-co… …etal forks for guests to track their dippers. Wooden or bamboo skewers c… …used, especially for dessert fondue.

4. Hea… …ivet

…pot on a sturdy trivet to protect your table from heat.

5. …apkins

…es, napkins, and plenty of bowls for sauces, dips, or used skewers.

Fondue Safety Tips

- …**flames.** Never leave Sterno or gel fuel burners unattended. Use …of surfaces and away from curtains or flammable items.
- …**om-temperature ingredients** for oil fondue. Moisture causes splattering.
- …**t double dip!** Keep things hygienic, especially in group settings.
- **Test oil temperature carefully.** Too hot, and food burns or splashes. Aim for 350°F (175°C) and use a thermometer if needed.
- **Keep children and pets away** from hot pots and skewers.
- **Extinguish flames properly.** Use the snuffer cap that comes with Sterno or gel fuel cans.
- **Don't overfill the pot.** Leave space for dippers and bubbling.

Clean-Up Tips

- Soak cheese pots right away to prevent crusting.
- Wipe chocolate pots with a spatula first, then wash with warm water.
- For oil pots, let oil cool completely, then strain or dispose of it properly (never pour down the sink).

With the right equipment and a little care, fondue is not only safe but incredibly fun. Think of your pot as a small, joyful centerpiece—a gathering place for flavor, warmth, and connection.

Chapter 1
Cheese Fondues

1. Classic Swiss Cheese Fondue

Time: 20 minutes

This is the gold standard of cheese fondue—smooth, creamy, and rich with the flavor of traditional alpine cheeses.

Ingredients:

- 1 clove garlic, halved
- 1 cup dry white wine (like Sauvignon Blanc)
- 1½ cups grated Gruyère cheese, 1½ cups grated Emmental cheese
- 1 tsp lemon juice
- 1 tbsp cornstarch
- 2 tbsp kirsch (optional)
- Freshly ground black pepper and a pinch of nutmeg

Instructions:

1. Rub the inside of your fondue pot with the garlic halves, then discard or mince them for stronger flavor.

2. Heat the wine and lemon juice in the pot over medium heat until steaming, not boiling.

3. Gradually add the cheese, stirring constantly in a figure-eight motion until melted.

4. Mix cornstarch and kirsch (or a bit of wine) into a smooth slurry, then stir it into the cheese to thicken.

5. Season with pepper and nutmeg. Keep warm over a low flame and stir occasionally to prevent sticking.

Best Dippers: Cubed baguette, steamed broccoli, apple slices, soft pretzels.

2. Cheddar Ale Fondue

Time: 20 minutes

This bold, flavorful twist uses sharp cheddar and a splash of your favorite ale for a rich, pub-style fondue. It's great for game night or hearty dinners.

Ingredients:

- 1 clove garlic, minced
- 1 cup lager or pale ale (not too bitter)
- 3 cups shredded sharp cheddar cheese
- 1 tbsp Worcestershire sauce
- 1 tsp dry mustard
- 2 tsp cornstarch
- 1 tbsp cold water

Instructions:

1. In a saucepan or fondue pot, sauté garlic in a touch of oil until fragrant.
2. Add the beer and bring to a gentle simmer.

3. Gradually stir in the cheddar cheese until smooth.
4. Mix cornstarch and water into a slurry, then stir into the pot to thicken.
5. Stir in Worcestershire sauce and dry mustard. Adjust to taste.

Best Dippers: Soft pretzel bites, smoked sausage, cauliflower florets, rye bread cubes.

3. Gruyère & Emmental Blend

Time: 20 minutes

This is the most authentic "moitié-moitié" fondue—half Gruyère, half Emmental. It's slightly nuttier and silkier than the classic version.

Ingredients:

- 1 clove garlic, halved
- 1 cup dry white wine
- 1½ cups grated Gruyère
- 1½ cups grated Emmental
- 1 tbsp lemon juice
- 1 tbsp cornstarch
- 2 tbsp kirsch (optional)
- White pepper, to taste

Instructions:

1. Rub the pot with garlic, then discard or chop for extra intensity.
2. Heat wine and lemon juice on medium-low until steaming.

3. Slowly add the cheeses, stirring in a zigzag or figure-eight pattern to avoid clumping.
4. Mix cornstarch with kirsch or wine and stir into the pot.
5. Season with white pepper and keep warm for dipping.

Best Dippers: Rustic bread cubes, blanched asparagus, pickles, roasted potatoes.

4. Fontina & White Wine Fondue

Time: 15 minutes

Fontina is creamy, mild, and melts like a dream. This version is silky and subtle—perfect for those who enjoy a gentler cheese flavor.

Ingredients:

- 2 cups grated Fontina cheese
- ¾ cup dry white wine
- 1 clove garlic, minced
- 1 tbsp cornstarch
- 1 tbsp water
- Salt and pepper, to taste

Instructions:

1. Heat the garlic and wine in the pot until hot but not boiling.
2. Add the Fontina gradually, stirring continuously to melt evenly.
3. Mix cornstarch and water into a slurry and add to the cheese to thicken.

4. Season with salt and pepper to taste.

Best Dippers: Pear slices, focaccia cubes, steamed green beans, artichoke hearts.

5. Brie & Mushroom Fondue

Time: 25 minutes

Earthy mushrooms and rich Brie make this a luxurious and slightly decadent option. Ideal for a cold night or a romantic meal.

Ingredients:

- 1 tbsp butter
- 1 cup finely chopped mushrooms (cremini or button)
- 1 clove garlic, minced
- 1 cup dry white wine
- 1½ cups Brie, rind removed and cubed
- 1 cup grated mozzarella or Fontina
- 1 tbsp cornstarch
- 1 tbsp water
- Fresh thyme or rosemary (optional)

Instructions:

1. In the fondue pot, melt butter and sauté mushrooms and garlic until soft and browned.

2. Add wine and bring to a gentle simmer.
3. Stir in the Brie and mozzarella, melting until smooth.
4. Whisk together cornstarch and water, then stir into the cheese.
5. Add fresh herbs if desired. Keep warm while serving.

Best Dippers: Sourdough chunks, sautéed mushrooms, cherry tomatoes, roasted carrots.

6. Smoky Gouda & Bacon Fondue

Time: 25 minutes

This deeply flavorful fondue combines smoked gouda with crispy bacon, offering a rich, comforting experience that feels like a hug in a bowl. It's ideal for cool-weather gatherings or as a bold starter for a dinner party.

Ingredients:

- 4 strips bacon, finely chopped
- 1 garlic clove, minced
- 1 cup dry white wine
- 2½ cups grated smoked gouda
- ½ cup cream cheese or mascarpone
- 1 tbsp cornstarch
- 1 tbsp water
- Black pepper, to taste
- Optional: chopped chives or parsley for garnish

Instructions:

1. Cook bacon in the fondue pot or a skillet until crispy. Remove and set aside, leaving a little fat in the pot.
2. Add garlic and wine to the pot and bring to a gentle simmer.
3. Slowly add gouda and cream cheese, stirring until melted and smooth.
4. Stir together cornstarch and water, then add to the cheese to thicken.
5. Fold in bacon and season with black pepper. Garnish if desired.

Best Dippers: Potato wedges, pretzel bites, roasted Brussels sprouts, grilled kielbasa.

7. Blue Cheese & Walnut Fondue

Time: 20 minutes

For lovers of bold, tangy flavors, this fondue blends creamy blue cheese with toasted walnuts for depth and texture. Serve it as an upscale appetizer or a statement dish during wine night.

Ingredients:

- 1 cup dry white wine
- 1½ cups shredded mozzarella or cream cheese
- ¾ cup crumbled blue cheese (like Gorgonzola or Roquefort)
- ½ tsp lemon juice
- 1 tbsp cornstarch
- 1 tbsp water
- ⅓ cup chopped toasted walnuts
- Fresh ground black pepper

Instructions:

1. Heat wine and lemon juice in the fondue pot until warm.

2. Slowly stir in mozzarella and blue cheese until melted and creamy.
3. Mix cornstarch with water and add to the pot, stirring until thickened.
4. Fold in toasted walnuts and season with pepper to taste.

Best Dippers: Pear slices, crusty baguette, roasted sweet potatoes, celery sticks.

8. Italian Four-Cheese Fondue

Time: 20 minutes

Bring a taste of Italy to your fondue night with this luxurious blend of mozzarella, Parmesan, provolone, and ricotta. It's smooth, savory, and perfect for dipping fresh bread and grilled veggies.

Ingredients:

- 1 cup whole milk
- 1½ cups shredded mozzarella
- ½ cup grated Parmesan
- ½ cup shredded provolone
- ¼ cup ricotta cheese
- 1 clove garlic, minced
- 1 tbsp cornstarch
- 2 tbsp cold water
- Salt and pepper, to taste

- Optional: chopped basil or oregano

Instructions:

1. Heat milk and garlic in the fondue pot until warm but not boiling.
2. Slowly stir in mozzarella, Parmesan, provolone, and ricotta, letting each melt before adding the next.
3. Stir cornstarch and water together, then mix into the pot until smooth and thickened.
4. Season to taste and add herbs if using.

Best Dippers: Garlic breadsticks, grilled zucchini, cherry tomatoes, focaccia.

9. Mexican Queso-Style Fondue

Time: 15 minutes

Inspired by Tex-Mex queso dip, this spicy and creamy fondue adds chili heat and bold flavor. It's a crowdpleaser perfect for parties and casual get-togethers.

Ingredients:

- 1 tbsp butter
- 1 small onion, finely diced
- 1 jalapeño, minced (seeds removed for less heat)
- 1 clove garlic, minced
- 1 cup evaporated milk
- 2 cups shredded Monterey Jack cheese
- 1 cup shredded cheddar cheese
- 1 tbsp cornstarch
- 2 tbsp water
- ½ tsp cumin

- Optional: diced tomatoes, green chilies, or chopped cilantro

Instructions:

1. In the fondue pot, melt butter and sauté onion, garlic, and jalapeño until softened.
2. Stir in evaporated milk and bring to a simmer.
3. Add cheeses gradually, stirring until smooth.
4. Mix cornstarch and water and stir into the fondue to thicken.
5. Add cumin and any extras, adjusting seasoning as desired.

Best Dippers: Tortilla chips, chorizo sausage, mini quesadillas, bell pepper strips.

10. French Onion Cheese Fondue

Time: 30 minutes

This fusion of fondue and French onion soup delivers savory, caramelized flavor with every bite. Perfect with toasted bread and beefy sides.

Ingredients:

- 2 tbsp butter
- 1 large onion, thinly sliced
- 1 tsp sugar
- 1 clove garlic, minced
- ¾ cup dry white wine
- 1 cup beef broth
- 2 cups shredded Gruyère cheese, and 1 cup shredded Swiss or mozzarella
- 1 tbsp cornstarch
- 2 tbsp water
- Salt and pepper to taste

Instructions:

1. In the fondue pot, melt butter and slowly cook onions with sugar over low heat until golden and caramelized (about 15 minutes).
2. Add garlic, wine, and broth, bringing it to a simmer.
3. Add cheeses a bit at a time, stirring constantly.
4. Mix cornstarch and water into a slurry and stir in to thicken.
5. Season to taste and keep warm for serving.

Best Dippers: Sourdough toast, beef meatballs, sautéed mushrooms, roasted garlic cloves.

11. Broccoli Cheddar Fondue

Time: 20 minutes

A nod to classic broccoli cheddar soup, this fondue is comforting and creamy with a vegetal twist. It's both nostalgic and totally satisfying.

Ingredients:

- 1 tbsp butter
- ½ cup finely chopped broccoli (plus extra for dipping)
- 1 clove garlic, minced
- 1 cup milk or light cream
- 2 cups shredded sharp cheddar cheese
- ½ tsp Dijon mustard
- 1 tbsp cornstarch
- 2 tbsp water
- Salt and pepper

Instructions:

1. Melt butter in the fondue pot, then add broccoli and garlic. Cook until softened.
2. Pour in milk and bring to a gentle simmer.
3. Gradually stir in the cheddar until melted and smooth.
4. Mix cornstarch and water, then stir into the pot to thicken.
5. Add Dijon, salt, and pepper to taste.

Best Dippers: Steamed broccoli, bread cubes, baby carrots, soft pretzels.

12. Pesto & Parmesan Fondue

Time: 20 minutes

This bright, herby fondue is a celebration of Italian flavors. The punch of basil pesto and the sharpness of Parmesan make for a vibrant dip that's both savory and fresh.

Ingredients:

- 1 cup dry white wine
- 1½ cups shredded mozzarella
- 1 cup grated Parmesan
- ¼ cup prepared basil pesto
- 1 tbsp cornstarch
- 1 tbsp cold water
- Salt and black pepper, to taste

Instructions:

1. Heat wine in the fondue pot until steaming.
2. Add mozzarella and Parmesan slowly, stirring until melted and smooth.

3. Mix cornstarch and water, stir into the pot to thicken.
4. Add the pesto and stir gently until fully combined.
5. Season with salt and pepper if needed. Keep warm and serve.

Best Dippers: Sun-dried tomato bread, grilled zucchini, cherry tomatoes, gnocchi.

13. Creamy Havarti Fondue

Time: 15 minutes

Havarti melts beautifully into a silky, mild cheese fondue. This one's perfect for those who enjoy a gentler, buttery flavor and a melt-in-your-mouth texture.

Ingredients:

- 1 clove garlic, halved
- 1 cup whole milk
- 2½ cups grated Havarti
- 1 tsp lemon juice
- 1 tbsp cornstarch
- 1 tbsp water
- Fresh nutmeg or white pepper, to taste

Instructions:

1. Rub garlic inside the pot, then discard.
2. Warm milk and lemon juice in the pot over medium-low heat.

3. Gradually stir in Havarti until melted.
4. Mix cornstarch and water, stir in to thicken the fondue.
5. Add a pinch of nutmeg or white pepper for a touch of warmth.

Best Dippers: Fresh apple slices, rye crackers, poached shrimp, soft sourdough.

14. Beer & Garlic Cheese Fondue

Time: 20 minutes

This hearty, pub-style fondue combines bold cheddar with the hoppy edge of beer and a hit of garlic. It's especially good for game nights or chilly evenings.

Ingredients:

- 1 tbsp butter
- 2 garlic cloves, minced
- 1 cup amber beer or lager
- 2 cups sharp cheddar, grated
- 1 cup shredded gouda or mozzarella
- 1 tbsp Dijon mustard
- 1 tbsp cornstarch
- 1 tbsp cold water
- Black pepper, to taste

Instructions:

1. In the pot, melt butter and sauté garlic until fragrant.
2. Pour in beer and bring to a low simmer.
3. Stir in cheddar and gouda gradually, mixing until smooth.
4. Stir mustard into the melted cheese.
5. Mix cornstarch and water, stir in to thicken.
6. Season with black pepper and keep warm.

Best Dippers: Pretzel bites, bratwurst slices, roasted cauliflower, onion rings.

15. Spicy Pepper Jack Fondue

Time: 15 minutes

For those who like a little kick, this fondue uses spicy pepper jack cheese and green chilies for a southwestern-style twist. It's bold, lively, and totally addictive.

Ingredients:

- 1 cup milk or evaporated milk
- 2½ cups shredded pepper jack cheese
- ¼ cup diced green chilies (canned or fresh)
- ½ tsp cumin
- 1 tbsp cornstarch
- 1 tbsp water
- Salt to taste

Instructions:

1. Heat the milk in the pot until just beginning to bubble.
2. Slowly add the pepper jack, stirring constantly.

3. Stir in chilies and cumin.
4. Combine cornstarch and water, then stir into the fondue to thicken.
5. Season with salt if needed.

Best Dippers: Tortilla strips, roasted sweet potato cubes, chicken tenders, jicama sticks.

16. Herb & Goat Cheese Fondue

Time: 20 minutes

Tangy and earthy, this elegant fondue features creamy goat cheese with fresh herbs. It's great for brunches, light dinners, or a sophisticated gathering.

Ingredients:

- ¾ cup dry white wine
- 1½ cups shredded mozzarella or cream cheese
- ¾ cup crumbled goat cheese
- 1 tbsp chopped fresh thyme or rosemary
- 1 tbsp cornstarch
- 2 tbsp water
- Salt and pepper to taste

Instructions:

1. Heat wine in the fondue pot until hot.
2. Gradually add mozzarella and goat cheese, stirring to melt.

3. Stir in chopped herbs.
4. Mix cornstarch and water, add to thicken.
5. Season and keep warm.

Best Dippers: Roasted beets, toasted baguette, figs, grilled eggplant slices.

17. Truffle Mac & Cheese Fondue

Time: 25 minutes

This indulgent recipe turns everyone's favorite comfort food into fondue. Creamy cheeses and a drizzle of truffle oil give it a decadent flair.

Ingredients:

- 1 cup whole milk or cream
- 1½ cups cheddar cheese, shredded
- 1 cup fontina, shredded
- ½ cup cream cheese
- 1 tbsp Dijon mustard
- 1 tbsp truffle oil (plus more for garnish)
- 1 tbsp cornstarch
- 2 tbsp water
- Salt to taste

Instructions:

1. Heat milk in the pot until warm.
2. Add cheddar, fontina, and cream cheese in batches, stirring until melted.
3. Stir in Dijon and truffle oil.
4. Mix cornstarch and water, stir in to thicken.
5. Garnish with an extra drizzle of truffle oil.

Best Dippers: Mini pasta shells, garlic bread, steamed broccolini, grilled mushrooms.

18. Swiss & Caramelized Leek Fondue

Time: 30 minutes

Caramelized leeks lend a subtle sweetness and sophistication to classic Swiss cheese, making this fondue rich, mellow, and elegant.

Ingredients:

- 1 tbsp butter
- 1 large leek, thinly sliced (white and light green parts)
- 1 cup dry white wine
- 1½ cups shredded Gruyère
- 1 cup shredded Swiss cheese
- 1 tbsp cornstarch
- 2 tbsp cold water
- Salt and pepper to taste

Instructions:

1. Melt butter in the pot and cook leeks slowly until soft and golden, about 10–12 minutes.

2. Add wine and bring to a simmer.
3. Gradually stir in both cheeses until smooth.
4. Mix cornstarch and water, add to the fondue.
5. Season to taste and keep warm.

Best Dippers: Roasted potatoes, sourdough, asparagus spears, seared sausage rounds.

19. Mediterranean Feta & Olive Fondue

Time: 15 minutes

Inspired by bold Mediterranean flavors, this unique fondue pairs creamy cheeses with briny olives and the tang of feta for a sunny, savory dip.

Ingredients:

- 1 cup whole milk
- 1½ cups shredded mozzarella
- ¾ cup crumbled feta
- ¼ cup chopped kalamata olives
- 1 tbsp olive oil
- 1 tbsp cornstarch
- 1 tbsp lemon juice
- Black pepper, to taste

Instructions:

1. Heat milk and lemon juice in the fondue pot.

2. Stir in mozzarella and feta until melted.
3. Add olives and olive oil, stir well.
4. Mix cornstarch with a bit of water or wine, stir into fondue to thicken.
5. Season with black pepper.

Best Dippers: Pita wedges, grilled zucchini, cucumber slices, grape tomatoes.

20. Applewood Smoked Cheddar Fondue

Time: 20 minutes

This rich, smoky fondue is a comforting favorite that pairs wonderfully with roasted vegetables and hearty bread. Applewood smoked cheddar adds complexity and depth.

Ingredients:

- 1 cup apple cider or dry white wine
- 2½ cups shredded applewood smoked cheddar
- 1 tbsp whole grain mustard
- 1 tbsp cornstarch
- 2 tbsp cold water
- Fresh thyme (optional)
- Salt and pepper to taste

Instructions:

1. Heat cider or wine in the pot until steaming.
2. Stir in cheddar gradually, stirring until smooth.

3. Add mustard and thyme (if using).
4. Mix cornstarch and water, stir into the cheese mixture to thicken.
5. Adjust seasoning and serve warm.

Best Dippers: Roasted apple slices, rye bread, grilled chicken bites, sweet potato fries.

Chapter 2
Chocolate Fondues

21. Classic Milk Chocolate Fondue

Time: 10 minutes

Simple, smooth, and beloved by all, this classic milk chocolate fondue is the heart of any dessert fondue night. Its creamy sweetness pairs perfectly with fruit, pastries, and marshmallows.

Ingredients:

- 1 cup heavy cream
- 2½ cups chopped milk chocolate or chocolate chips
- 1 tsp vanilla extract
- Pinch of salt

Instructions:

1. Heat the cream in your fondue pot or saucepan until just beginning to steam—do not boil.

2. Add the chopped milk chocolate and stir gently until melted and smooth.

3. Stir in vanilla and salt. Keep warm over low heat while serving.

Best Dippers: Strawberries, banana slices, pound cake, graham crackers, marshmallows.

22. Dark Chocolate & Sea Salt Fondue

Time: 10 minutes

This grown-up twist on fondue features rich dark chocolate and a hit of sea salt. Slightly bitter, slightly sweet, and deeply indulgent, it's perfect for those who love bold flavors.

Ingredients:

- 1 cup heavy cream
- 2 cups chopped dark chocolate (60–70% cacao)
- 1 tbsp honey or maple syrup (optional, for sweetness)
- ½ tsp vanilla extract
- Flaky sea salt for garnish

Instructions:

1. Warm cream in the fondue pot over medium-low heat.
2. Add dark chocolate and stir until fully melted.
3. Mix in honey (if using) and vanilla.

4. Sprinkle with flaky sea salt just before serving.

Best Dippers: Fresh figs, orange slices, biscotti, toasted almonds, dried apricots.

23. White Chocolate Raspberry Swirl

Time: 12 minutes

This elegant and visually striking fondue pairs sweet white chocolate with a tart raspberry swirl. It's creamy, fruity, and an absolute showstopper.

Ingredients:

- ¾ cup heavy cream
- 2 cups chopped white chocolate or chips
- ⅓ cup raspberry jam or fresh raspberry purée
- 1 tsp lemon juice

Instructions:

1. In a small saucepan or fondue pot, heat cream until hot but not boiling.
2. Stir in white chocolate and melt until smooth.
3. In a separate bowl, stir the jam with lemon juice.
4. Spoon raspberry mixture on top of the fondue and swirl lightly with a skewer.

Best Dippers: Strawberries, ladyfingers, angel food cake, pineapple chunks.

24. Hazelnut Chocolate Fondue

Time: 10 minutes

A rich, nutty favorite that tastes like a melted chocolate-hazelnut spread. It's kid approved, adult-loved, and almost impossible to stop eating.

Ingredients:

- ¾ cup heavy cream
- 1½ cups milk chocolate chips
- ½ cup chocolate-hazelnut spread (like Nutella)
- ½ tsp vanilla extract

Instructions:

1. Warm cream in the pot over medium heat.
2. Add chocolate chips and stir until melted.
3. Mix in the hazelnut spread and vanilla, whisking until silky and uniform.

Best Dippers: Waffles, strawberries, apple slices, biscotti, pretzel sticks.

25. Salted Caramel Chocolate Fondue

Time: 15 minutes

This indulgent recipe blends chocolate and caramel into a luscious, glossy sauce with just a hint of salt. It's luxurious and festive—perfect for holidays or celebrations.

Ingredients:

- ¾ cup caramel sauce (store-bought or homemade)
- ¾ cup heavy cream
- 2 cups chopped semi-sweet or dark chocolate
- ½ tsp sea salt, plus more to taste

Instructions:

1. In the fondue pot, warm caramel sauce and cream together over low heat.
2. Stir in chocolate until melted and smooth.
3. Add sea salt and adjust to taste.

Best Dippers: Apple slices, cinnamon cookies, donut holes, roasted pecans.

26. Mint Chocolate Chip Fondue

Time: 10 minutes

Cool and creamy, this fondue brings the flavor of mint chocolate chip ice cream into molten form. It's fun, refreshing, and surprisingly light.

Ingredients:

- ¾ cup heavy cream
- 2 cups chopped semi-sweet chocolate
- ½ tsp peppermint extract
- ½ cup mini chocolate chips (for sprinkling)
- Optional: a drop of green food coloring for a minty hue

Instructions:

1. Heat cream until steaming.
2. Add chocolate and stir until melted.
3. Stir in peppermint extract and food coloring if using.
4. Just before serving, sprinkle in chocolate chips for texture.

Best Dippers: Chocolate cookies, brownie bites, marshmallows, frozen banana chunks.

27. Cookies & Cream Fondue

Time: 12 minutes

This fondue is as fun as it sounds—melted white chocolate base loaded with crushed chocolate sandwich cookies. It's a guaranteed crowdpleaser for kids and adults alike.

Ingredients:

- ¾ cup heavy cream
- 2 cups chopped white chocolate
- 1 tsp vanilla extract
- 6 chocolate sandwich cookies, crushed

Instructions:

1. Warm cream in the fondue pot.
2. Stir in white chocolate and melt until fully smooth.
3. Mix in vanilla and half the crushed cookies.
4. Sprinkle the remaining cookies on top before serving.

Best Dippers: More sandwich cookies, mini donuts, strawberries, graham cracker sticks.

28. Mocha Espresso Chocolate Fondue

Time: 12 minutes

Mocha lovers rejoice—this fondue is a sophisticated blend of deep chocolate and aromatic espresso. It's the perfect finish to a dinner party or a rich indulgence on a cozy night in.

Ingredients:

- ¾ cup heavy cream
- 2 cups chopped dark chocolate or semi-sweet chips
- 2 tsp instant espresso powder
- 1 tbsp Kahlúa or brewed coffee (optional)
- ½ tsp vanilla extract

Instructions:

1. Heat the cream in the fondue pot until steaming.
2. Stir in chocolate and espresso powder. Continue stirring until completely melted.
3. Mix in Kahlúa and vanilla. Stir well until glossy and uniform.

Best Dippers: Chocolate biscotti, ladyfingers, strawberries, dried cherries.

29. Peanut Butter Chocolate Fondue

Time: 10 minutes

This rich, creamy combo brings together two iconic flavors—chocolate and peanut butter. It's comforting, decadent, and a massive hit with kids and adults alike.

Ingredients:

- 1 cup heavy cream
- 2 cups milk chocolate chips
- ½ cup smooth peanut butter
- Pinch of salt
- 1 tsp vanilla extract

Instructions:

1. Warm the cream in your fondue pot.
2. Add chocolate and stir until nearly melted.
3. Add peanut butter and salt. Stir until silky smooth.
4. Mix in vanilla and keep warm over low heat.

Best Dippers: Pretzel sticks, banana slices, marshmallows, graham crackers, apple wedges.

30. Coconut Chocolate Fondue

Time: 10 minutes

This tropical twist infuses rich chocolate with coconut milk and flakes. Creamy and exotic, it makes a dreamy dessert after a spicy meal or beach-themed party.

Ingredients:

- 1 cup canned full-fat coconut milk
- 2 cups chopped dark or milk chocolate
- 1 tsp coconut extract (optional)
- ¼ cup toasted shredded coconut

Instructions:

1. Heat the coconut milk in the fondue pot until warm.
2. Add chocolate and stir until fully melted.
3. Stir in coconut extract for a boost of flavor.
4. Sprinkle toasted coconut on top before serving.

Best Dippers: Pineapple chunks, shortbread cookies, mango slices, macaroons.

31. Orange Zest Dark Chocolate Fondue

Serves: 4

Time: 12 minutes

This elegant fondue pairs dark chocolate with the fresh brightness of orange. It's fragrant, rich, and perfect with simple fruits or buttery cakes.

Ingredients:

- 1 cup heavy cream
- 2 cups chopped dark chocolate
- Zest of 1 orange
- 2 tbsp orange liqueur (such as Grand Marnier, optional)
- Pinch of sea salt

Instructions:

1. Warm cream in the fondue pot, then add chocolate.
2. Stir until melted and silky.
3. Mix in orange zest, liqueur, and salt. Stir well and keep warm.

Best Dippers: Orange segments, pound cake, dried apricots, strawberries.

32. Strawberry Cheesecake Fondue

Serves: 4

Time: 15 minutes

This fondue is like dipping into your favorite dessert. White chocolate and cream cheese come together in a luscious base swirled with strawberry preserves.

Ingredients:

- ¾ cup heavy cream
- 1½ cups chopped white chocolate
- ½ cup cream cheese, softened
- ⅓ cup strawberry preserves
- 1 tsp lemon juice

Instructions:

1. Heat cream in the pot until warm.
2. Stir in white chocolate and melt until smooth.
3. Mix in cream cheese and lemon juice until fully incorporated.

4. Swirl in strawberry preserves just before serving.

Best Dippers: Cheesecake bites, graham crackers, fresh strawberries, vanilla wafers.

33. Chocolate Churro Fondue

Serves: 4

Time: 12 minutes

This cinnamon-kissed chocolate fondue gives off strong churro vibes with none of the frying. A warm, sweet-spicy dip that pairs best with crunchy or soft textures.

Ingredients:

- 1 cup heavy cream
- 2 cups semi-sweet chocolate
- 1 tsp ground cinnamon
- 2 tbsp brown sugar
- Pinch of cayenne (optional)
- ½ tsp vanilla extract

Instructions:

1. In the pot, heat cream, cinnamon, and sugar until warm.
2. Add chocolate and stir until melted.

3. Stir in vanilla and cayenne for extra warmth.

Best Dippers: Cinnamon donuts, churro sticks, puff pastry pieces, fried plantains.

34. Almond Joy Fondue

Serves: 4

Time: 15 minutes

Inspired by the classic candy bar, this fondue blends chocolate, coconut, and almonds into a dreamy dessert dip with both creamy and crunchy notes.

Ingredients:

- ¾ cup coconut milk
- 2 cups milk chocolate chips
- ¼ cup shredded coconut
- ¼ cup chopped roasted almonds
- ½ tsp almond extract

Instructions:

1. Warm the coconut milk in the fondue pot.
2. Add chocolate and melt while stirring.
3. Stir in coconut, almonds, and almond extract.

4. Keep warm and stir before each dip to evenly distribute bits.

Best Dippers: Marshmallows, graham crackers, macaroons, dried banana chips.

35. Chocolate Marshmallow Fondue

Serves: 4

Time: 10 minutes

This playful fondue turns melted chocolate and gooey marshmallow fluff into a nostalgic, s'mores-inspired dream. It's sticky, fun, and always a hit with kids.

Ingredients:

- ¾ cup heavy cream
- 2 cups milk chocolate
- 1 cup marshmallow fluff or crème
- 1 tsp vanilla extract

Instructions:

1. Warm cream in the pot and add chocolate. Stir until smooth.
2. Mix in marshmallow fluff and vanilla until fully blended.
3. Stir well and keep warm, reheating gently if it thickens.

Best Dippers: Graham crackers, Rice Krispie treats, brownie chunks, banana slices.

36. S'mores-Inspired Fondue

Time: 15 minutes

This fondue brings together all the elements of classic s'mores—chocolate, marshmallow, and a touch of smoky graham goodness—in a single pot.

Ingredients:

- 1 cup heavy cream
- 2 cups chopped semi-sweet chocolate
- 1 cup mini marshmallows or marshmallow fluff
- 1 tsp vanilla
- Crushed graham crackers for topping

Instructions:

1. Heat cream in the fondue pot.
2. Add chocolate and stir until melted.
3. Mix in marshmallows or fluff and stir gently.
4. Sprinkle crushed graham crackers over the top and serve warm.

Best Dippers: Graham crackers, toasted marshmallows, chocolate chip cookies, fruit slices.

36. S'mores-Inspired Fondue

Time: 15 minutes

Everything you love about s'mores—gooey marshmallow, melted chocolate, and crunchy graham crackers—gets melted into a cozy, crowd-pleasing fondue. It's great for camping nights or indoor fun.

Ingredients:

- 1 cup heavy cream
- 2 cups semi-sweet chocolate chips
- 1 cup mini marshmallows (or ½ cup marshmallow fluff)
- 1 tsp vanilla extract
- ¼ cup crushed graham crackers

Instructions:

1. Heat the cream in the fondue pot until hot but not boiling.
2. Stir in the chocolate and melt until smooth.
3. Add marshmallows or fluff and stir gently until fully blended.
4. Stir in vanilla and top with crushed graham crackers before serving.

Best Dippers: Graham crackers, marshmallows, brownie cubes, banana slices, strawberries.

37. Black Forest Cherry Fondue

Serves: 4

Time: 15 minutes

This rich chocolate fondue is inspired by Black Forest cake. The combination of dark chocolate and cherry creates a luxurious dessert with a hint of romance and decadence.

Ingredients:

- ¾ cup heavy cream
- 2 cups dark chocolate chips or chopped dark chocolate
- ½ cup cherry pie filling or cherry preserves
- 1 tbsp cherry liqueur (Kirsch), optional
- Whipped cream or extra cherries for garnish

Instructions:

1. In your fondue pot, heat the cream until steaming.
2. Stir in dark chocolate until melted and smooth.
3. Add the cherry filling and liqueur (if using), mixing gently to combine.

4. Serve with a dollop of whipped cream or a cherry on top for presentation.

Best Dippers: Pound cake, chocolate cookies, fresh cherries, biscotti.

38. Banana Split Chocolate Fondue

Serves: 4

Time: 10 minutes

This fondue captures the joy of a banana split in a single pot—chocolate, bananas, strawberries, and a hint of vanilla come together for a fun, ice-cream-parlor-inspired dessert.

Ingredients:

- ¾ cup heavy cream
- 2 cups milk chocolate chips
- 1 mashed ripe banana
- ½ tsp vanilla extract
- ½ cup diced strawberries (optional)

Instructions:

1. Heat cream in the fondue pot.
2. Add the mashed banana and stir to combine.
3. Stir in chocolate until fully melted and smooth.

4. Add vanilla and fold in strawberries just before serving.

Best Dippers: Banana chunks, pineapple, waffle pieces, vanilla cake cubes, cherries.

39. Pumpkin Spice White Chocolate Fondue

Serves: 4

Time: 12 minutes

Perfect for autumn or Thanksgiving, this cozy fondue blends smooth white chocolate with pumpkin purée and classic pumpkin spice. It's warm, sweet, and wonderfully seasonal.

Ingredients:

- ¾ cup heavy cream
- 2 cups chopped white chocolate
- ½ cup canned pumpkin purée
- 1 tsp pumpkin pie spice
- ½ tsp cinnamon
- Pinch of salt

Instructions:

1. In your fondue pot, heat cream, pumpkin, and spices until warm.
2. Stir in white chocolate and melt gently, stirring until smooth.

3. Add a pinch of salt to balance sweetness.

Best Dippers: Gingersnaps, graham crackers, apple slices, cinnamon rolls, biscotti.

40. Holiday Peppermint Bark Fondue

Serves: 4

Time: 10 minutes

This festive fondue turns classic peppermint bark into a warm, melty dip perfect for winter celebrations. The cooling peppermint and creamy chocolate make a refreshing combo.

Ingredients:

- ¾ cup heavy cream
- 2 cups semi-sweet or dark chocolate chips
- ½ tsp peppermint extract
- ¼ cup crushed candy canes or peppermint candies

Instructions:

1. Heat the cream in the fondue pot until steaming.
2. Add chocolate and stir until melted and smooth.
3. Stir in peppermint extract.
4. Sprinkle crushed candy canes on top before serving.

Best Dippers: Sugar cookies, brownie bites, pretzels, shortbread, marshmallows.

Chapter 3
Broth & Oil Fondues

41. Classic Beef Broth Fondue (Fondue Bourguignonne)

This traditional style uses hot beef broth to cook bite-sized pieces of beef, chicken, or vegetables. It's light, flavorful, and perfect with a spread of dipping sauces.

Ingredients:

- 4 cups beef broth
- 1 clove garlic, minced
- 1 tbsp Worcestershire sauce
- 1 tsp soy sauce
- Salt and black pepper, to taste

Instructions:

1. In your fondue pot, bring the beef broth to a simmer.

2. Add garlic, Worcestershire, soy sauce, salt, and pepper.
3. Transfer the pot to its heat source and keep it at a gentle simmer.
4. Skewer raw beef, mushrooms, or vegetables and cook them directly in the hot broth for 2–4 minutes, depending on thickness.

Best Dippers: Cubed sirloin, zucchini rounds, baby potatoes, dipping sauces like horseradish cream, chimichurri, and aioli.

42. Garlic & Herb Broth Fondue

Infused with fresh herbs and garlic, this aromatic broth is ideal for chicken, shrimp, or firm vegetables. It's a great choice for a lighter fondue night.

Ingredients:

- 4 cups chicken or vegetable broth
- 3 cloves garlic, crushed
- 2 sprigs rosemary
- 2 sprigs thyme
- 1 bay leaf
- Zest of 1 lemon
- Salt and pepper

Instructions:

1. Simmer broth with garlic, herbs, lemon zest, salt, and pepper for 10 minutes.
2. Strain out the solids if desired, or leave herbs in for a rustic touch.
3. Keep the broth at a simmer in the fondue pot.

4. Dip pieces of chicken, shrimp, or vegetables and cook until tender.

Best Dippers: Chicken breast strips, shrimp, bell pepper chunks, pearl onions, yogurt-based dips or herb vinaigrette.

43. Spicy Asian Broth Fondue

Packed with ginger, soy sauce, and a kick of chili, this flavorful broth is perfect for cooking thin cuts of meat and vegetables with an Asian twist.

Ingredients:

- 4 cups low-sodium beef or chicken broth
- 1-inch piece fresh ginger, sliced
- 2 cloves garlic, crushed
- 2 tbsp soy sauce
- 1 tbsp rice vinegar
- 1 tsp sesame oil
- ½ tsp red pepper flakes
- 1 green onion, chopped

Instructions:

1. Combine all ingredients in the pot and bring to a simmer.
2. Cook for 5–10 minutes to allow flavors to blend.
3. Transfer to the burner and keep simmering throughout the meal.

4. Thinly sliced steak or mushrooms cook in just 1–2 minutes.

Best Dippers: Beef slices, tofu, snap peas, shiitake mushrooms, ponzu sauce or sweet chili dip.

44. Tomato Basil Broth Fondue

A tangy tomato-based broth with the sweetness of basil makes for a Mediterranean-inspired fondue experience. Ideal with chicken, fish, or veggies.

Ingredients:

- 4 cups chicken broth
- 1 cup tomato purée
- 2 tbsp olive oil
- 2 cloves garlic, minced
- 1 tsp dried oregano
- 1 tsp sugar
- ¼ cup chopped fresh basil or 1 tsp dried
- Salt and pepper

Instructions:

1. Sauté garlic in olive oil, then add the rest of the ingredients.
2. Bring to a gentle boil, then reduce to simmer for 10 minutes.

3. Transfer to fondue pot and keep warm.

4. Cook shrimp, chicken, or veggies directly in the broth.

Best Dippers: Chicken, zucchini, cherry tomatoes, mozzarella cubes, pesto mayo or balsamic glaze for dipping.

45. Thai Coconut Broth Fondue

Creamy, spicy, and fragrant, this coconut-based broth is inspired by Thai soups. It's especially delicious for seafood and tofu.

Ingredients:

- 1 can (13.5 oz) coconut milk
- 2 cups chicken or vegetable broth
- 1 stalk lemongrass, crushed
- 1 tbsp red curry paste
- 1 tsp fish sauce or soy sauce
- 1 tbsp lime juice
- 1-inch piece ginger, sliced

Instructions:

1. Combine all ingredients in a pot and bring to a simmer.
2. Let it simmer for 10–15 minutes to infuse flavors.
3. Pour into fondue pot and keep warm.

4. Skewer raw shrimp, tofu, or vegetables and cook gently in the hot broth.

Best Dippers: Shrimp, scallops, baby corn, tofu cubes, coconut-peanut sauce or chili-lime dip.

46. Mushroom Vegetable Broth Fondue

A vegetarian favorite, this deeply savory broth
uses mushrooms and aromatics to add umami to every dip.

Ingredients:

- 4 cups vegetable broth
- 1 cup sliced mushrooms (shiitake, cremini, or button)
- 1 small onion, chopped
- 2 cloves garlic, minced
- 1 tbsp soy sauce
- 1 bay leaf
- Black pepper, to taste

Instructions:

1. Sauté onion and garlic until fragrant. Add mushrooms and cook until softened.
2. Add broth, soy sauce, bay leaf, and pepper. Simmer for 10 minutes.
3. Pour into fondue pot and keep warm over a burner.

4. Use to cook tofu, vegetables, and dumplings.

Best Dippers: Cauliflower florets, dumplings, mushrooms, tofu, teriyaki sauce or miso dressing.

47. Sesame Soy Oil Fondue

This oil-based fondue is great for cooking thin slices of meat or seafood with a nutty, umami flavor base. It's bold and sizzling.

Ingredients:

- 2 cups canola or peanut oil
- 1 tbsp sesame oil
- 2 tbsp soy sauce
- 2 garlic cloves, sliced
- 1 green onion, chopped

Instructions:

1. Heat all ingredients together in a pan.
2. Transfer to a metal fondue pot and place over a burner.
3. Keep the oil hot but not smoking (around 350°F).
4. Dip small pieces of beef or shrimp into the oil using fondue forks, cooking for 1–2 minutes.

Best Dippers: Beef strips, scallops, bell pepper wedges, soy-ginger sauce or hoisin dip.

48. Mediterranean Olive Oil Fondue

This herb-infused olive oil is excellent for lamb, chicken, and vegetables. The flavors are subtle but sophisticated.

Ingredients:

- 2 cups light olive oil or grapeseed oil
- 2 cloves garlic, sliced
- 1 tsp dried oregano
- 1 sprig rosemary
- Zest of ½ lemon
- Pinch of red pepper flakes

Instructions:

1. Heat all ingredients together until warm and aromatic.
2. Transfer to fondue pot and heat over burner to maintain a hot cooking temperature.
3. Skewer lamb cubes or veggies and fry until golden.

Best Dippers: Lamb cubes, eggplant, mushrooms, pita chips, tzatziki or olive tapenade.

49. Cajun-Style Oil Fondue

Spicy and bold, this southern-style oil fondue is perfect for chicken, sausage, and shrimp. It delivers heat and flavor in every dip.

Ingredients:

- 2 cups peanut oil
- 1 tsp paprika
- 1 tsp cayenne pepper
- ½ tsp garlic powder
- ½ tsp onion powder
- 1 tsp Cajun seasoning blend

Instructions:

1. Combine all ingredients in a metal fondue pot and heat until hot (350°F).
2. Skewer raw chicken, sausage, or shrimp and cook in the hot oil.
3. Serve with spicy dipping sauces or remoulade.

Best Dippers: Andouille sausage, chicken strips, okra slices, cornbread cubes.

50. Red Wine & Rosemary Broth Fondue

A rich and elegant choice, this wine-infused broth is ideal for beef or pork. The rosemary adds a subtle herbal note that elevates the dish.

Ingredients:

- 2 cups beef broth
- 1½ cups dry red wine
- 1 sprig rosemary
- 2 cloves garlic, smashed
- 1 small shallot, sliced
- Salt and black pepper

Instructions:

1. Combine all ingredients and simmer for 10–15 minutes.
2. Strain out solids if desired, then transfer to fondue pot.
3. Skewer thin beef slices and cook until just pink in the center.

Best Dippers: Beef tenderloin, mushroom caps, pearl onions, horseradish sauce or red wine reduction.

Chapter 4

Creative Dessert & Specialty Fondues

51. Dulce de Leche Fondue

Sweet, thick, and utterly luscious, this caramel-based fondue is a dream for anyone with a love for Latin desserts. Its creamy texture and deep flavor pair beautifully with fresh fruit and buttery pastries.

Ingredients:

- 1 can (14 oz) sweetened condensed milk
- ½ cup heavy cream
- 1 tsp vanilla extract
- Pinch of salt

Instructions:

1. In a fondue pot or saucepan, heat the condensed milk and cream over low heat, stirring constantly.

2. Once smooth and warm, add vanilla and a pinch of salt.
3. Stir until everything is well blended and glossy.
4. Keep warm over low heat while serving.

Best Dippers: Apple slices, churros, shortbread, banana chunks, waffle pieces.

52. Maple Cinnamon Fondue

Perfect for chilly fall mornings or festive brunches, this fondue features the warmth of cinnamon and the rich sweetness of maple syrup. It feels like dipping into a melted cinnamon roll.

Ingredients:

- ¾ cup heavy cream
- 1 cup white chocolate chips
- ¼ cup pure maple syrup
- 1 tsp ground cinnamon
- ½ tsp vanilla extract

Instructions:

1. Warm the cream in your fondue pot over medium heat.
2. Stir in the white chocolate chips until melted and smooth.
3. Add maple syrup, cinnamon, and vanilla.
4. Stir gently until everything is fully blended and fragrant.

Best Dippers: French toast cubes, apple slices, cinnamon graham crackers, mini pancakes.

53. Lemon Curd Fondue

Bright, tangy, and refreshingly smooth, this fondue is a citrusy contrast to heavier desserts. It's great as a light, zesty ending to any meal.

Ingredients:

- ¾ cup lemon curd (store-bought or homemade)
- ½ cup heavy cream
- 2 tbsp unsalted butter
- 1 tsp lemon zest

Instructions:

1. In a saucepan or fondue pot, combine lemon curd, cream, and butter over low heat.
2. Stir gently until melted and combined.
3. Add lemon zest and stir until glossy.
4. Keep warm and serve with fresh or sweet dippers

Best Dippers: Strawberries, graham crackers, angel food cake, blueberries, vanilla wafers.

54. Matcha White Chocolate Fondue

This elegant green-hued fondue pairs the earthy flavor of matcha with creamy white chocolate. It's a visually striking and delicately flavored dessert ideal for tea lovers.

Ingredients:

- ¾ cup heavy cream
- 2 cups white chocolate chips
- 1 tbsp matcha powder
- ½ tsp vanilla extract
- Pinch of salt

Instructions:

1. Heat the cream in your fondue pot until just below boiling.
2. Whisk in matcha powder until smooth.
3. Add white chocolate and stir gently until melted.
4. Mix in vanilla and salt. Stir until glossy and well blended.

Best Dippers: Mochi, coconut macaroons, almond cookies, melon cubes, marshmallows.

55. Champagne Chocolate Fondue

Elegant and celebratory, this bubbly twist on chocolate fondue is perfect for New Year's Eve, anniversaries, or romantic evenings. The champagne adds a gentle fruitiness that balances dark chocolate beautifully.

Ingredients:

- ¾ cup champagne or sparkling wine
- 2 cups dark or semi-sweet chocolate, chopped
- 1 tsp vanilla extract
- 1 tbsp butter

Instructions:

1. In your fondue pot, heat champagne until steaming but not boiling.
2. Stir in chocolate slowly, allowing it to melt smoothly.
3. Add butter and vanilla, stirring until silky and glossy.
4. Keep warm over a low flame.

Best Dippers: Strawberries, madeleines, shortbread, macarons, ladyfingers.

56. Apple Cider Caramel Fondue

A fall favorite, this sweet-tart caramel fondue is infused with apple cider for depth and warmth. It's perfect for cozy evenings or Halloween parties.

Ingredients:

- ¾ cup apple cider
- ½ cup heavy cream
- 1½ cups soft caramels or caramel bits
- 1 tbsp butter
- Pinch of cinnamon and salt

Instructions:

1. Combine cider and cream in the fondue pot. Heat over medium, stirring gently.
2. Add caramels and stir constantly until melted and smooth.
3. Stir in butter, cinnamon, and salt.
4. Keep warm and stir occasionally while serving.

Best Dippers: Green apple slices, spice cookies, donut holes, pears, soft pretzels.

57. Nutella Cream Fondue

Velvety and nutty, this ultra-easy fondue uses the iconic chocolate-hazelnut spread. It's quick, satisfying, and perfect when you want something rich without much prep.

Ingredients:

- 1 cup Nutella
- ½ cup heavy cream
- 1 tsp vanilla extract
- Pinch of sea salt

Instructions:

1. Warm cream in the fondue pot over medium-low heat.
2. Stir in Nutella and mix until melted and smooth.
3. Add vanilla and salt, then stir until well blended.
4. Keep warm and serve with a mix of sweet and salty dippers.

Best Dippers: Strawberries, pretzels, croissants, marshmallows, chocolate chip cookies.

58. Pistachio Vanilla Fondue

Nutty, creamy, and sophisticated, this fondue combines the earthy richness of pistachios with the warm sweetness of vanilla. It's a unique, elegant choice for those looking to surprise their guests with something special.

Ingredients:

- ¾ cup heavy cream
- 2 cups white chocolate chips
- ¼ cup pistachio paste or finely ground pistachios
- 1 tsp vanilla extract
- Pinch of salt

Instructions:

1. Heat the cream in your fondue pot until steaming.
2. Stir in the white chocolate until melted and smooth.
3. Add pistachio paste and vanilla. Stir until well blended and glossy.
4. Add a pinch of salt to enhance flavor.

Best Dippers: Biscotti, poached pears, almond cookies, strawberries, shortbread.

59. Honey Lavender Fondue

Floral and delicately sweet, this fondue brings a calming, almost tea-like quality to dessert. It's perfect for springtime gatherings, bridal showers, or when you want something light and beautiful.

Ingredients:

- ¾ cup heavy cream
- 1½ cups chopped white chocolate
- 2 tbsp honey
- 1 tsp dried culinary lavender
- ½ tsp lemon zest (optional)

Instructions:

1. Warm cream with lavender in your fondue pot. Let steep for 5 minutes.
2. Strain out lavender and return cream to the pot.
3. Add white chocolate and stir until smooth.
4. Stir in honey and lemon zest if using.

Best Dippers: Madeleines, angel food cake, blueberries, figs, vanilla wafers.

60. Birthday Cake Sprinkle Fondue

Bright, cheerful, and festive, this fun fondue turns any gathering into a party. With flavors of vanilla and cake batter, plus colorful sprinkles, it's sure to make kids (and adults) smile.

Ingredients:

- ¾ cup heavy cream
- 2 cups white chocolate chips
- 1 tsp butter
- 1 tsp vanilla extract
- ¼ cup rainbow sprinkles

Instructions:

1. Heat cream in the fondue pot until hot but not boiling.
2. Add white chocolate and butter, stirring until melted and smooth.
3. Stir in vanilla. Just before serving, fold in half the sprinkles and sprinkle the rest on top.

Best Dippers: Mini cupcakes, pound cake, animal crackers, strawberries, marshmallows.

Chapter 5
Light & Healthy Fondues

61. Light Yogurt & Dill Dip (Served Warm)

This tangy, herbaceous fondue makes a wonderful appetizer or side for grilled vegetables or lean meats. It's made with Greek yogurt, so it's creamy but packed with protein and light on fat.

Ingredients:

- 2 cups plain Greek yogurt
- 1 tbsp olive oil
- 1 tbsp chopped fresh dill
- 1 garlic clove, minced
- 1 tsp lemon juice
- Salt and pepper to taste

Instructions:

1. In your fondue pot, heat olive oil and garlic until fragrant.
2. Lower the heat and whisk in the yogurt.
3. Add lemon juice, dill, salt, and pepper.
4. Warm gently, stirring continuously, until the dip is heated through but not boiling.
5. Serve immediately with fresh or steamed veggies.

Best Dippers: Steamed carrots, cucumber slices, cherry tomatoes, grilled chicken skewers.

62. Steamed Veggie Broth Fondue

A clean, light broth is the perfect base for dipping vegetables, tofu, or lean seafood. This recipe is rich in flavor thanks to ginger, herbs, and lemon, yet easy on calories.

Ingredients:

- 4 cups low-sodium vegetable broth
- 1 inch fresh ginger, sliced
- 1 garlic clove, smashed
- 1 lemon, sliced
- 2 sprigs parsley or cilantro
- Salt and pepper

Instructions:

1. Simmer all ingredients together in a saucepan for 10–15 minutes.
2. Strain out solids if desired.
3. Pour into your fondue pot and keep at a steady simmer.
4. Cook vegetables or tofu until tender (about 1–2 minutes depending on size).

Best Dippers: Broccoli florets, zucchini, tofu cubes, snap peas, baby corn.

63. Lemon Herb Oil Fondue (with Lean Meats or Fish)

This light oil fondue uses olive oil and fresh herbs, making it ideal for lean proteins like white fish, shrimp, or chicken breast. It's elegant, simple, and heart-healthy.

Ingredients:

- 2 cups light olive oil
- Zest of 1 lemon
- 2 sprigs thyme or rosemary
- 1 garlic clove, crushed
- Pinch of chili flakes (optional)

Instructions:

1. Combine all ingredients in a saucepan and gently heat for 5–10 minutes to infuse flavor.
2. Pour into a metal fondue pot and place over a burner.
3. Use fondue forks to cook small bites of fish or chicken directly in the oil (about 2–3 minutes each).

Best Dippers: White fish cubes, shrimp, chicken breast, mushrooms, grape tomatoes.

64. Greek Yogurt Chocolate Fondue

Yes, you can have chocolate and still keep it light. This Greek yogurt-based fondue is tangy, creamy, and far less heavy than traditional cream-and-chocolate versions.

Ingredients:

- 1 cup plain Greek yogurt
- 1½ cups semi-sweet chocolate chips or chopped chocolate
- 1 tsp honey or maple syrup
- ½ tsp vanilla extract

Instructions:

1. Melt chocolate gently in the fondue pot over low heat.
2. Remove from heat and whisk in yogurt, honey, and vanilla.
3. Return to low heat to warm gently while serving. Avoid boiling to prevent curdling.

Best Dippers: Strawberries, banana slices, graham crackers, pineapple chunks.

65. Low-Fat Cheese & Tomato Fondue

This savory, lower-fat option blends reduced-fat cheese and tomato purée into a warm, Mediterranean-style dip. Great for veggies, whole grain bread, or grilled chicken.

Ingredients:

- 1 cup low-fat milk
- 1½ cups reduced-fat mozzarella or part-skim cheese, grated
- ½ cup tomato purée
- 1 garlic clove, minced
- 1 tbsp cornstarch mixed with 1 tbsp water
- Salt, pepper, and oregano

Instructions:

1. Heat milk and garlic in your fondue pot until warm.
2. Stir in tomato purée, then slowly add cheese, stirring constantly.
3. Add cornstarch mixture to thicken slightly.
4. Season with oregano, salt, and pepper. Stir until smooth.

Best Dippers: Whole grain bread cubes, grilled zucchini, turkey meatballs, red bell peppers.

These light and healthy fondues show that you can enjoy the comfort and fun of fondue without sacrificing your wellness goals. They're packed with fresh ingredients, lean proteins, and vibrant flavors, offering a guilt-free way to dip, share, and savor. Whether you're planning a light lunch, a post-workout dinner, or a wellness-inspired dinner party, these recipes will keep your fondue pot bubbling and your guests happy.

Chapter 6
Vegan & Dairy-Free Fondues

66. Cashew Cheese Fondue

Cashews create a creamy, cheesy texture without any dairy. This savory fondue is rich, nutty, and perfectly seasoned. A blender is essential here, but the rest is simple.

Ingredients:

- 1½ cups raw cashews (soaked for 4 hours or overnight)
- 1¼ cups water or unsweetened almond milk
- 2 tbsp nutritional yeast
- 1 tbsp lemon juice
- 1 clove garlic
- ½ tsp Dijon mustard
- Salt and pepper to taste

Instructions:

1. Drain and rinse the soaked cashews.

2. Blend all ingredients until completely smooth.

3. Pour the mixture into your fondue pot and warm gently, stirring frequently until thickened and hot.

4. Adjust seasoning as needed.

Best Dippers: Sourdough, broccoli, sweet potato cubes, apple slices.

67. Vegan Beer & Garlic Fondue

This recipe brings a bold, savory kick to your table. Made with plant-based cheese or a cashew base, the beer and garlic shine through, creating a pub-style experience.

Ingredients:

- 1 tbsp olive oil
- 2 cloves garlic, minced
- 1 cup beer (lager or ale)
- 1 cup unsweetened almond or soy milk
- 2 cups vegan shredded cheddar or cashew cheese sauce
- 1 tbsp arrowroot or cornstarch dissolved in 2 tbsp cold water
- 1 tsp lemon juice
- Black pepper to taste

Instructions:

1. In the fondue pot, sauté garlic in olive oil until soft.
2. Add beer and plant milk. Bring to a low simmer.

3. Slowly stir in vegan cheese or cashew sauce, stirring until smooth.

4. Stir in starch slurry to thicken. Add lemon juice and pepper.

Best Dippers: Soft pretzels, roasted cauliflower, vegan sausage slices, rye bread.

68. Almond Milk Chocolate Fondue

Smooth and luscious, this dairy-free chocolate fondue uses almond milk and dark vegan chocolate to create a simple yet luxurious dessert.

Ingredients:

- 1 cup unsweetened almond milk
- 2 cups vegan dark chocolate chips or chopped chocolate
- 1 tsp vanilla extract
- 1 tbsp maple syrup (optional)

Instructions:

1. Heat almond milk in your fondue pot until warm.
2. Stir in chocolate and melt slowly over low heat.
3. Add vanilla and sweetener if needed. Stir until glossy.

Best Dippers: Strawberries, bananas, vegan cookies, pretzels, dried apricots.

69. Coconut Caramel Dessert Fondue

This plant-based caramel sauce uses coconut milk and coconut sugar to create a rich, toasty, dairy-free dip. It's thick, sweet, and full of flavor.

Ingredients:

- 1 cup full-fat coconut milk
- ¾ cup coconut sugar or brown sugar
- 1 tbsp coconut oil
- ½ tsp vanilla extract
- Pinch of sea salt

Instructions:

1. Combine coconut milk and sugar in your fondue pot over medium heat.
2. Stir until sugar is dissolved, then simmer gently for 10–12 minutes until thickened.
3. Stir in coconut oil, vanilla, and salt.
4. Keep warm and stir occasionally while serving.

Best Dippers: Apple slices, pineapple chunks, vegan pound cake, cinnamon tortilla chips.

70. Dairy-Free Thai Peanut Fondue

This savory, nutty fondue brings the bold flavors of Thai cuisine into the spotlight. It's creamy, spicy, and completely dairy-free.

Ingredients:

- 1 cup full-fat coconut milk
- ½ cup smooth natural peanut butter
- 1 tbsp soy sauce or tamari
- 1 tbsp lime juice
- 1 tsp fresh ginger, grated
- 1 tsp maple syrup
- Crushed peanuts or chili flakes (optional garnish)

Instructions:

1. Combine all ingredients in your fondue pot.
2. Warm over medium-low heat, whisking constantly until smooth.
3. Garnish with crushed peanuts or chili flakes if desired.

Best Dippers: Grilled tofu, bell pepper strips, cucumber slices, sweet potato wedges, rice crackers.

With these five dairy-free recipes, everyone gets to enjoy the magic of fondue, no matter their dietary needs. Creamy, bold, and deeply satisfying, these plant-based alternatives prove that fondue is for everyone. Whether you're celebrating, hosting friends, or enjoying a quiet night at home, these vegan-friendly options make every dip a delight.

Chapter 7
Mastering the Melt

Perfect Pairings

Fondue is about more than just what goes in the pot. The beauty of fondue lies in the full experience—what you dip, sip, and serve alongside it. Whether you're planning an intimate evening or a festive get-together, pairing the right ingredients, beverages, and accompaniments will elevate your fondue from simple to sensational.

In this chapter, we'll guide you through thoughtful pairings for cheese, chocolate, broth, and oil fondues. We'll explore dippers, drinks, and side dishes that complement each style, along with tips to balance flavors and textures.

Cheese Fondue Pairings

Cheese fondue is rich, creamy, and comforting. Its intense flavor calls for balance—think crusty, chewy, crisp, and slightly sweet.

Best Dippers:

- **Bread:** Baguette, sourdough, rye, pretzel bites, multigrain cubes
- **Vegetables:** Steamed broccoli, cauliflower, baby potatoes, cherry tomatoes, asparagus
- **Fruits:** Apples, pears, grapes (especially with stronger cheeses)
- **Proteins:** Sliced bratwurst, ham cubes, grilled chicken
- **Extras:** Roasted garlic cloves, sun-dried tomatoes, pickles

Drink Pairings:

- **White wines** like Sauvignon Blanc, Pinot Grigio, or Riesling cut through the richness
- **Light red wines** such as Pinot Noir for heartier cheese blends
- **Crisp lagers or wheat beers** go beautifully with cheddar or gouda fondues
- **Sparkling water** with lemon or herbs for a refreshing non-alcoholic option
- **Side Ideas:**
- Arugula salad with lemon vinaigrette

- Roasted nuts or marinated olives
- Herb focaccia or grissini breadsticks

Chocolate Fondue Pairings

Chocolate fondue is indulgent, sweet, and smooth. The key is to offer a variety of textures—from juicy to crunchy, soft to chewy—to keep each dip exciting.

Best Dippers:

- **Fruits:** Strawberries, banana slices, pineapple, orange wedges, cherries, apple slices
- **Sweets:** Marshmallows, pound cake cubes, mini donuts, pretzels, cookies, biscotti
- **Savories:** Bacon strips or sea salt crackers (for a bold twist)

Drink Pairings:

- **Port wine** or a sweet red blend complements chocolate's richness
- **Espresso or coffee** enhances mocha or dark chocolate fondues
- **Champagne** adds celebration and contrast
- **Flavored milk** or hot cocoa for kids

Side Ideas:

- Whipped cream, chopped nuts, or crushed candy for topping
- Ice cream scoops served on the side
- A light fruit salad to balance sweetness

Broth Fondue Pairings

Broth-based fondues (like Fondue Chinoise) are lighter, more savory, and offer a cook-at-the-table experience. They pair best with fresh vegetables, thin meats, and dipping sauces that build layers of flavor.

Best Dippers:

- **Proteins:** Thin slices of beef, chicken breast, pork loin, shrimp, scallops
- **Vegetables:** Mushrooms, zucchini, carrots, bok choy, broccoli, baby corn
- **Dumplings or noodles:** Small potstickers, rice noodles, or udon (added after cooking)

Dipping Sauces:

- Garlic butter

- Soy-ginger glaze
- Horseradish cream
- Cilantro-lime dressing
- Spicy peanut or sesame sauce

Drink Pairings:

- **Dry white wines** (like Grüner Veltliner or Chardonnay) balance broth's saltiness
- **Sake or soju** for Asian-style broths
- **Light beers** like pilsner or rice lager
- **Lemon-infused water** or iced tea for a clean, hydrating option

Side Ideas:

- Steamed rice or couscous
- Pickled vegetables
- Fresh herb salad

Oil Fondue Pairings

Oil fondues are rich and hearty, perfect for small cuts of meat and seafood. Pairings should help balance the fat with brightness, crunch, or acidity.

Best Dippers:

- **Meats:** Beef tenderloin, chicken, pork, lamb cubes, sausage slices
- **Seafood:** Shrimp, scallops, calamari rings
- **Veggies:** Zucchini, sweet potatoes, mushrooms (all firm enough to fry)

Batter Options: Light tempura, beer batter, or seasoned flour coating for extra crunch

Dipping Sauces:

- Garlic aioli
- Cajun mayo
- Tartar sauce for seafood
- Mustard dill sauce
- Spicy ketchup or barbecue glaze

Drink Pairings:

- **Full-bodied red wines** like Cabernet or Zinfandel
- **Amber ales** or IPAs for hearty meats
- **Sparkling wine** for contrast
- **Cucumber lemonade** or citrus spritzers as refreshing non-alcoholic options

Side Ideas:

- Coleslaw or shredded cabbage salad
- Roasted vegetable skewers
- Toasted bread with dipping oils

Mix & Match Tips

You don't have to stick to one fondue type per meal. Try a **three-course fondue dinner**:

1. **Start with a cheese fondue** as a warm appetizer
2. **Move to broth or oil fondue** for the main course, allowing everyone to cook their own bites
3. **Finish with chocolate or a specialty dessert fondue** for a sweet ending

Add in a few **signature cocktails or mocktails**, offer **sauce flights**, and display your dippers in colorful, artful arrangements for a truly memorable experience.

Fondue Flavor Balancing Tips

- **Rich cheese?** Add tart fruit, pickles, or crusty bread
- **Sweet chocolate?** Use salty dippers like pretzels or bacon
- **Spicy broth?** Cool it down with cucumber dip or rice
- **Greasy oil fondue?** Add fresh greens or a tangy slaw on the side

Fondue is a playground of flavor. With the right pairings, every dip becomes an adventure, every bite balanced and beautiful. Whether you lean sweet or savory, bold or subtle, pairing thoughtfully is the secret to fondue success. And best of all—it's as fun to build your own combinations as it is to eat them.

Troubleshooting

Common Fondue Issues and How to Fix Them

Fondue is a wonderful, interactive dining experience, but like any cooking method, it can present a few hiccups along the way. Whether you are dealing with a cheese fondue that turns gritty or a chocolate fondue that thickens too fast, the good news is that almost every problem has a simple fix. This chapter walks you through the most common fondue mishaps and teaches you how to solve them on the spot.

1. The Cheese Fondue is Lumpy or Gritty

The problem:

Your cheese fondue looks curdled or separates into oily clumps. This is one of the most common issues and usually happens when the cheese is overheated or not properly emulsified.

The fix:

- Always **grate cheese finely** before adding. Large chunks melt unevenly.
- **Add cheese slowly**, over low heat, and stir continuously in a zigzag or figure-eight motion.
- Make sure there is **enough acid** in the base. Dry white wine and lemon juice help prevent clumping by keeping the proteins in the cheese stable.
- If the fondue becomes gritty, remove it from heat and stir in **a splash of lemon juice or white wine**. Then stir in **1 to 2 teaspoons of cornstarch** dissolved in cold wine. This can help rebind the mixture.

Prevention tips:

Use melting cheeses like Gruyère, Fontina, Emmental, or Havarti. Always keep the heat low once the cheese starts to melt.

2. The Chocolate Fondue is Too Thick

The problem:

Your chocolate fondue is too stiff or starts to clump. It may be difficult to dip fruits or marshmallows properly.

The fix:

- Stir in **a little more cream or milk**, one tablespoon at a time, until it reaches the desired consistency.

- Avoid using water to thin chocolate, as it can cause seizing. Stick to cream or milk with some fat content.
- Add **a bit of butter** to improve texture and shine.

Prevention tips:

Warm the cream first, then slowly add chocolate. Always melt chocolate over low heat. Avoid overheating or using too little liquid.

3. The Chocolate Fondue is Grainy or Seized

The problem:

Instead of a smooth pool of melted chocolate, your fondue has turned gritty and dry. This happens when a small amount of water gets into melted chocolate or when chocolate is overheated.

The fix:

- Try stirring in **1 tablespoon of heavy cream or vegetable oil** at a time to bring it back.
- You can also stir in **a small amount of warm milk or melted butter** gradually to restore smoothness.
- If it is beyond repair, it may be best to start over with fresh chocolate.

Prevention tips:

Always use dry utensils and bowls when working with chocolate. Avoid any steam from boiling water if using a double boiler.

4. The Fondue Burns at the Bottom

The problem:

Your fondue is sticking or burning at the bottom of the pot, giving it a scorched flavor.

The fix:

- Stir frequently and avoid letting the flame or heat source get too strong.
- Scrape gently with a wooden spoon to prevent sticking, not a metal utensil.
- If it is already scorched, carefully pour the unburnt portion into a clean pot without disturbing the burnt bottom.

Prevention tips:

Use a **low flame or a temperature-controlled electric fondue pot**. Always start with a gentle heat and stir regularly.

5. Ingredients Are Not Cooking Fast Enough in Broth or Oil

The problem:

Meats or vegetables are taking too long to cook in the broth or oil, which can slow down the meal and frustrate guests.

The fix:

- **Check the heat source**. The liquid may not be hot enough. For broth, maintain a steady simmer. For oil, keep it around 350°F (use a cooking thermometer if needed).
- **Cut food smaller and thinner**. Smaller cuts cook faster and more evenly.
- Make sure you are not overcrowding the pot, which can reduce the heat.

Prevention tips:

Preheat the broth or oil thoroughly before bringing it to the table. Have a lid handy to cover the pot if the temperature needs to rise.

6. The Oil Is Smoking or Overheating

The problem:

If your oil fondue is releasing smoke or smells burnt, it has likely overheated. This can be dangerous and also affect the taste of the food.

The fix:

- Remove the pot from the heat immediately. Let it cool slightly before returning it to a lower setting.
- Discard oil that has developed a burnt smell or dark color and start with fresh oil.
- Use a **neutral oil with a high smoke point**, such as canola, peanut, or sunflower oil.

Prevention tips:

Keep oil temperature below 375°F. Never walk away from an active burner, and use a **metal fondue pot designed for hot oil** only.

7. Dippers Are Falling Off the Fork

The problem:

Bread or fruit keeps slipping off into the pot. This can be annoying and cause burns when trying to retrieve the lost piece.

The fix:

- Use **firmer bread** like sourdough or rustic baguette. Soft white bread often crumbles.

- For fruits, slice thick enough to stay secure.
- Skewer items closer to the center for better grip. You can also use two-pronged fondue forks designed for better hold.

Prevention tips:

Dry the surface of fruit before dipping. Avoid overloading the fork with heavy or slippery items.

8. Guests Are Double-Dipping or Sharing Forks

The problem:

You want to maintain good hygiene, especially when sharing food with a group.

The fix:

- **Provide personal plates** for each guest to transfer melted cheese or chocolate onto.
- Offer **extra wooden skewers or dipping forks** so that guests can use one fork to dip and another to eat.
- Give a friendly reminder at the start of the meal if needed.

Prevention tips:

Set the table with individual sauce bowls and napkins. Have plenty of skewers or tongs available.

9. The Fondue Is Cooling Too Fast

The problem:

Your fondue keeps thickening or losing heat, making it harder to enjoy over time.

The fix:

- Stir regularly to keep the heat evenly distributed.
- Make sure the heat source is stable and not too weak.
- For cheese or chocolate, a small tea light or electric warming base works well.
- For broth or oil, use gel fuel burners or electric bases that maintain steady cooking temperatures.

Prevention tips:

Warm the pot before adding ingredients, and choose a fondue pot appropriate for your recipe (ceramic for cheese and chocolate, stainless steel for oil and broth).

10. You Made Too Much (or Too Little)

The problem:

You either overestimated or underestimated how much fondue to make.

The fix:

- If you made too much cheese or chocolate, **refrigerate leftovers in an airtight container**. Cheese can often be reheated with a splash of wine or milk.
- If you made too little, keep **extra shredded cheese, chocolate, or broth ingredients on hand** to quickly make another batch.
- You can also stretch your fondue by **offering more dippers** and serving side dishes.

Prevention tips:

Plan on about 1/3 to 1/2 cup of fondue per person for cheese and chocolate, and 1 to 1½ cups of broth or oil for main courses.

Fondue can seem intimidating at first, but once you learn how to fix the most common mistakes, it becomes easy and enjoyable. Most problems are minor and can be solved with a few simple adjustments. With a little patience and the right tips, your fondue night will be smooth, delicious, and fun from the first dip to the last.

Get Your Free E-book

Get Your Free E-book
Scan the QR code below to instantly access the e-book
'The Fondue Host's Cheat Sheet', absolutely free

SCAN ME

https://bonus.grapevinebooks.com/fonduecheatsheet